HOW'S YOUR HEALTH?

Colds, the Flu, and Other Infections

Angela Royston

A⁺

Smart Apple Media

Smart Apple Media is published by Black Rabbit Books
P.O. Box 3263, Mankato, Minnesota 56002

Printed in the United States

Published by arrangement with the Watts Publishing Group Ltd, London.

Editor: Sarah Eason
Design: Paul Myerscough
Illustration: Annie Boberg and Geoff Ward
Picture research: Sarah Jameson
Consultant: Dr. Stephen Earwicker

Acknowledgements:
The publisher would like to thank the following for permission to reproduce photographs: Alamy p.10, p.16, p.19, p.20; Istockphoto p.7; CMSP p.11, p.25; Inmagine p.13, p.26; Tudor Photography p.8, p.15, p.22, p.23, p.27; Chris Fairclough Photography p.6, p.9, p.12, p.14, p.17, p.18, p.21, p.24.

Library of Congress Cataloging-in-Publication Data

Royston, Angela.
    Colds, the flu, and other infections / Angela Royston.
    p. cm.—(Smart Apple Media. How's your health?)
    Summary: "Describes the causes, symptoms, treatment of colds and flu, and how to prevent them"—Provided by publisher.
    Includes index.
    ISBN 978-1-59920-217-4
    1. Cold (Disease)—Juvenile literature. 2. Influenza—Juvenile literature. I. Title. II. Series.
RF361.R693 2009
616.2'05—dc22   2007035699

9 8 7 6 5 4 3 2 1

Contents

What Are Colds and the Flu?

Colds and the flu are illnesses that affect your throat, nose, and chest.

If you have a cold, you will probably sneeze and have a sore throat, a runny nose, and a cough. A cold lasts between one and two weeks.

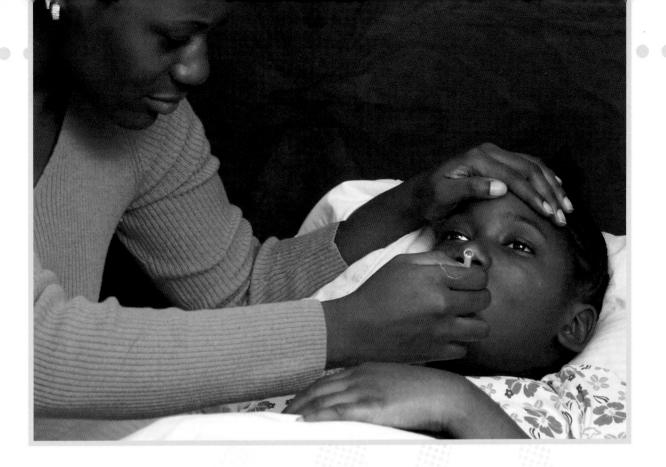

The flu is worse than a cold because your muscles ache and you feel tired. You also have a **fever**. This means that your body becomes much hotter than usual, yet you may shiver and feel cold at the same time.

Why Do You Shiver When You Have a Fever?

The air around you feels cold when you have a fever because your body is hot. Shivering is its way of trying to warm up, even though it needs to cool down!

Why Do Colds and the Flu Affect Your Breathing?

When you have a cold or the flu, thick liquid called **mucus** may give you a stuffy nose. The mucus makes it hard to **breathe**.

When you have a cold or the flu, your nose and some **airways** in your **lungs** become filled with mucus. Your nose may be so full of thick mucus—or snot—that you cannot breathe through it.

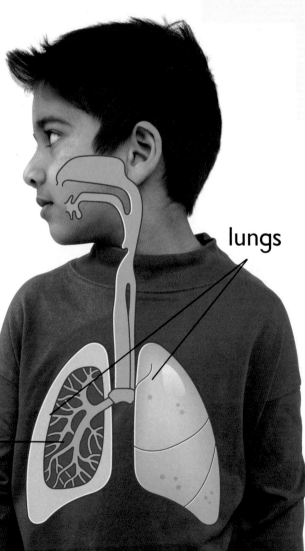

lungs

airway

Colds and the flu can also make people cough. Coughing is the body's way of getting rid of anything that might be blocking the airways.

Tickly coughs are caused by swelling in your throat. The swelling makes your body think that your throat is blocked, which is why you cough. Chest coughs are caused by mucus in your lungs. When you cough, the mucus is loosened.

What Causes Colds and the Flu?

Very tiny **germs** called **viruses** cause colds and the flu.

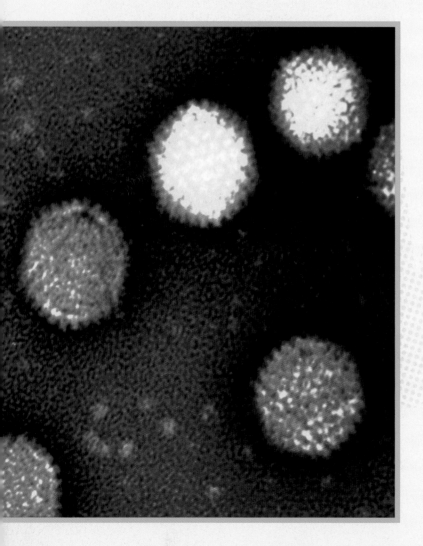

A virus is so small it can be seen only under a microscope. A microscope is a machine that makes things look much bigger than they actually are. This is what a cold virus looks like under a powerful microscope.

Tiny Viruses

Viruses are the smallest living things—it would take two million of them to cover the head of a pin! They easily float through the air because they are so light.

Your airways are lined with tiny hairs and mucus. The hairs push mucus through the airway. This is what the tiny hairs look like under a microscope. Your body makes extra mucus when you have a cold or the flu. The extra mucus washes away germs inside your airways.

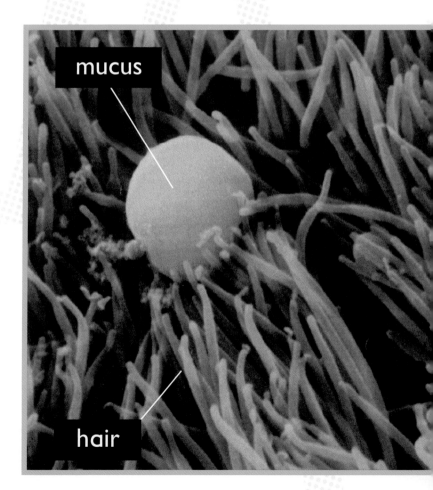

mucus

hair

How Are Colds and the Flu Treated?

Resting and drinking lots of water will help treat a cold or the flu.

When you have a cold, you should keep warm and drink plenty of water. You need to replace the water your body loses when making mucus. Putting a few drops of salty water in your nostrils can help clear your stuffy nose.

The flu can make you feel very sick. If you catch the flu, it is best to stay in bed. Sleeping will give your body a chance to deal with the illness.

How You Can Help

+ Drink lots of water.
+ Rest.
+ Stay in bed if you have the flu.

Which Medicines Help Treat Colds and the Flu?

Painkillers and cough medicine may make people feel better, but they don't cure a cold or the flu.

A painkiller stops your headache and makes your throat feel better. It can also help reduce a high **temperature**.

Take Care!

Only take medicine given to you by a parent or caregiver. It is important to carefully follow the instructions. People should never take more medicine than shown in the instructions, or another dose too soon after the last one.

Cough medicine helps stop coughing. Medicine for a tickly cough soothes the throat. Medicine for a chest cough helps clear mucus in the lungs.

15

How Are Colds and the Flu Caught?

The most usual way to catch a cold or the flu is by breathing in viruses through your nose or mouth.

When someone with a cold sneezes, germs spray into the air. They float in the air, and can easily be breathed in by someone else. Some viruses land on things around you. They cling to your fingers if you touch them.

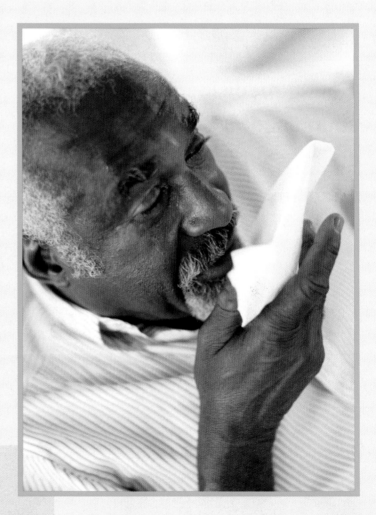

When someone with a cold coughs, germs spray into the air and you might breathe them in. Some germs can get on your fingers. If you touch your face, the germs can then get into your nose or mouth.

Try This!

Squirt water out of a water gun or an old dish soap bottle. How far does the water go? When you sneeze or cough, millions of germs shoot out your nose and mouth with just as much force!

Can You Stop Colds and the Flu from Spreading?

You can stop germs from spreading by covering your mouth and nose when you sneeze and cough. Washing your hands helps too.

Throw used tissues into a wastebasket. If you leave tissues lying around, germs on them can float into the air and give someone else a cold or the flu.

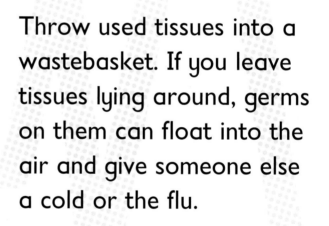

When you sneeze, cough, or blow your nose, lots of germs get on your hands. Wash your hands often so that you do not spread germs when you touch things.

How You Can Help

+ Cover your nose and mouth when you sneeze or cough.
+ Put used tissues into a wastebasket with a lid.
+ Wash your hands often.

Do Colds and the Flu Cause Other Illnesses?

Sometimes you may get a chest **infection** or ear infection after you have had a cold or the flu.

Ear infections and chest infections are often caused by germs called **bacteria**. This is what the bacteria that cause chest infections look like under a microscope.

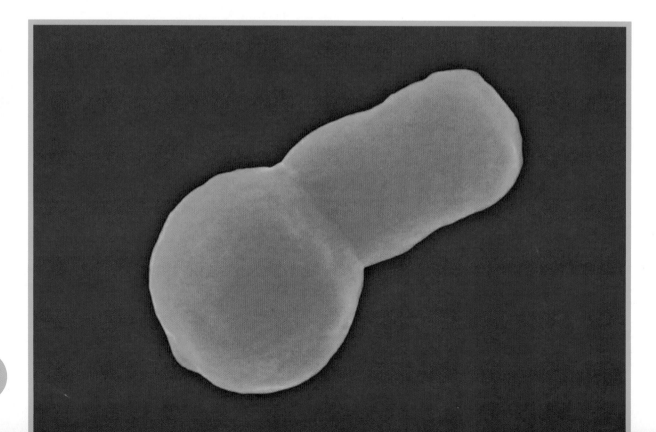

Bacteria

Bacteria are very small. Each one can split in half to make two bacteria. Each of those bacteria then split to make more bacteria. This is how a few bacteria can quickly become thousands of bacteria.

An ear infection can give you a very bad earache. It is caused by bacteria in your ear. A chest infection can lead to a bad cough and pain in your chest. This is caused by bacteria in your lungs.

How Do Doctors Treat Other Infections?

A doctor may give you medicine called an **antibiotic** to kill the bacteria that cause infection.

Antibiotics are special medicines that you usually swallow. Antibiotics kill the bacteria that cause infections, but they cannot kill viruses.

When you take an antibiotic, it is very important that you follow the instructions. You may feel better after a few days, but you must keep taking the antibiotic for as long as your doctor tells you.

Take Care!

Antibiotics should only be taken if given by a doctor. It is important to follow the doctor's instructions. If too little medicine is taken, it will not kill all the bacteria. If the antibiotics are stopped too soon, some of the bacteria will keep living and could make people sick again.

What Is an Upset Stomach?

When you have an upset stomach, you may be sick or have **diarrhea**.

An upset stomach is caused by germs in your stomach. Germs get into your stomach through your mouth. Germs can live on food or on something you put in your mouth. They can also float in the air. People sometimes get an upset stomach when they have a cold or the flu.

You should always wash your hands after using the bathroom and before eating food. Washing your hands washes away the germs that can cause an upset stomach.

How You Can Help

+ Drink plenty of water. The water will replace liquid lost by being sick or having diarrhea.
+ Eat only plain food, such as salted crackers and plain rice. Plain food is easier on your stomach.

How Can You Prevent Colds and the Flu?

You are less likely to catch a cold or the flu if you keep your body healthy.

Eat healthy food, such as lots of fruits and vegetables. Healthy food helps your body work well, which means it can deal with colds, the flu, and other infections.

How You Can Help

+ Eat plenty of fruits and vegetables.
+ Drink eight cups of water every day.
+ Get plenty of exercise that gets your heart pumping.
+ Wash your hands after using the bathroom and before eating or drinking.
+ Get plenty of sleep.

You are more likely to get sick when you are very tired. Sleep allows your body time to recover, and this helps you stay well. People sleep best when they go to bed at about the same time each night. Adults need to sleep about eight hours. Children need to sleep longer.

Glossary

airway   tube in the lungs through which air passes.

antibiotic   medicine that kills bacteria.

bacteria   tiny living things, some of which can make you sick.

breathe   to take in and let out air through the mouth and nose.

diarrhea   when the solid waste your body makes is loose and runny.

fever   when an infection makes your body temperature higher than usual.

germ   tiny living thing that can make you sick.

infection   illness caused by germs.

lung   part of the body that breathes in and breathes out air.

mucus   thick liquid made by the body. Mucus comes out of your nose when it is runny.

painkiller   medicine that stops you feeling pain.

temperature   how hot or cold something is. When you have a temperature, your body is much hotter than usual.

virus   germ. Some viruses cause colds and the flu.

Find Out More

Chilling Out with Colds
www.kidshealth.org/kid/ill_injure/sick/colds.html

Healthfinder.gov for Kids: Ways to Stay Healthy
and Have Fun
www.healthfinder.gov/kids

Infection Detection Prevention: How to
Keep from Getting Sick
www.amnh.org/nationalcenter/infection

Every effort has been made by the publisher to ensure that these Web sites contain no inappropriate or offensive material. However, because of the nature of the Internet, it is impossible to guarantee that the contents of these sites will not be altered. We strongly advise that Internet access is supervised by a responsible adult.

Index